GRIZZLY BEARS
of Alaska

Explore the Wild
World of Bears

Debbie S. Miller

Photography by Patrick J. Endres

little bigfoot

An imprint of Sasquatch Books | Seattle

Where rivers curl through mountains,
rushing to the sea,

you'll find Alaska's grizzlies,
roaming wild and free.

A Magnificent Creature

Alaska's most fierce land predator appears massive, from its huge tracks and three-inch claws, to its fortress of a body and **powerful jaws**. It's a grizzly bear! The hump above its muscular shoulders is unmistakable.

Grizzly bears live in wild, open country throughout Alaska. Some bears are blond or cinnamon in color, while others are dark brown. Their thick fur coat has **grizzled guard hairs** with pale tips, which give the bear its name.

Grizzlies have wide, round faces, small eyes and ears, and a long snout. They have an **excellent sense of smell** that is seven times stronger than a bloodhound's. Their nasal cavities are full of sensitive tissues that look like honeycomb, and cover a surface that is 100 times larger than the tissues inside a human nose. Studies have found that a grizzly can smell an animal carcass from miles away.

Brown Bear or Grizzly?

Some bears live along Alaska's central and southern coasts where they have a lush habitat and **mild climate**. While they are the same species as grizzlies, these coastal bears are known as brown bears. During the summer and fall, brown bears feed on a salad of plants, roots, berries, and a protein-rich diet of salmon. Some bears dig for clams and other creatures along the ocean shore with their **curved claws**.

Coastal brown bears grow much bigger than inland grizzlies because of the abundance of vegetation and salmon. A subspecies of the brown bear, the Kodiak Island brown bear, is even bigger! An adult male Kodiak brown bear can stand ten feet tall and weigh as much as 1,500 pounds, about the weight of 300 Chihuahuas. It is the world's largest omnivore.

Who's Hungry?

Grizzly bears are widespread in Interior Alaska and the Arctic. There, the density of grizzlies is much lower than along the coast. In the Arctic, there is one grizzly for every 300 square miles, compared to one brown bear per one square mile on the coast. Grizzlies live in a **harsh environment** with frigid winter temperatures and short summers, where food can be scarce.

Grizzly bears feed on a mixed diet of grasses, sedges, roots, insects, and berries. Like brown bears, grizzlies are **omnivores** because they eat plants and animals. They inhabit the land with other grazing animals such as wandering bull caribou. In the spring, grizzlies prey on the calves of moose and caribou. They also use the **powerful muscles** in their shoulders to dig up the tundra and turn over boulders to catch small rodents such as voles and lemmings or the Arctic ground squirrel.

Sik-Sik-Sik! When a grizzly bear approaches, a ground squirrel gives an alarm call to warn other squirrels of this dangerous predator. Then it scampers underground to hide in its burrow.

Leaving the Den

In the quiet cold of winter, grizzlies are snug underground in their **snow-covered dens**. In January or February, pregnant grizzlies give birth to tiny, hairless cubs that only weigh a pound. Within a few months, the cubs grow into fifteen-pound bundles of energy thanks to their mother's rich milk. Mother grizzlies usually have two cubs, but will sometimes give birth to three.

In Denali National Park, the warm spring sunshine melts the winter snow and the sweet smell of earth drifts through the air. After **seven months of hibernation**, the bears emerge from their dens. Mother grizzlies hungrily sniff and search for food in the mountain valleys while their cubs playfully follow them. They may discover old frozen cranberries or a leftover winter carcass of a moose. They also nibble on fresh green shoots of grasses and sedges.

Can't Catch Me!

Grizzly and brown bear cubs **love to play**. They wrestle, tumble, roll in the snow, and play with objects they discover. Siblings enjoy playing tag and tussling with each other.

Mother bears are very protective of their cubs. If they sense danger, they will huff at their cubs, urging them to climb trees for safety. Unlike the big and heavy adult bears, cubs are able to **climb trees** because of their light weight, agility, and sharp claws.

Ready for a Swim?

At dawn, a coastal brown bear mother is ready to **wade** and swim through the water in search of salmon. Her cubs **swim** behind her, observing where and how their mother fishes. The cubs stay with their mother for two to three years learning important **hunting skills**.

Got One!

Brown bears are **strong swimmers** and highly skilled at catching salmon. Sometimes they stand upright, like a human, looking for fish. They have **good vision** and can recognize different colors. This helps them clearly see the red salmon swimming through rivers.

A mother bear can duck underwater and snatch salmon with her powerful jaws. She will tear apart the fish with her **sharp teeth** and claws, and share it with her hungry cubs.

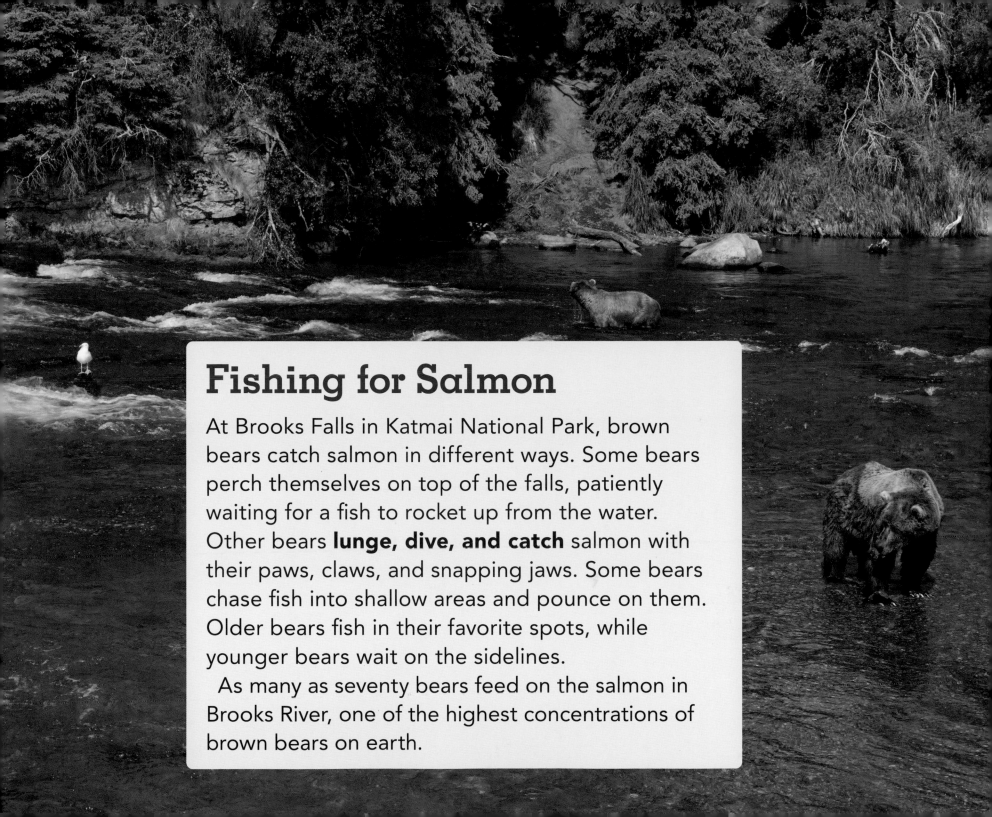

Fishing for Salmon

At Brooks Falls in Katmai National Park, brown bears catch salmon in different ways. Some bears perch themselves on top of the falls, patiently waiting for a fish to rocket up from the water. Other bears **lunge, dive, and catch** salmon with their paws, claws, and snapping jaws. Some bears chase fish into shallow areas and pounce on them. Older bears fish in their favorite spots, while younger bears wait on the sidelines.

As many as seventy bears feed on the salmon in Brooks River, one of the highest concentrations of brown bears on earth.

Fighting for Fish

After waiting patiently, an experienced brown bear can snatch a jumping salmon with its sharp teeth. When a bear walks off with its prize, other bears might fight over the **territory**. The stronger, dominant bear will roar and snap at the challenging bear. The smaller bear usually backs off, and the dominant bear can begin fishing.

During the peak of a salmon run, brown bears can consume as much as ninety pounds of fish in a day. This is equivalent to a bear eating about 162 cheeseburgers! Salmon are high in protein and rich with oil. This important food helps the bears build their fat reserves for the long winter. Some bears double their body weight prior to hibernation.

WARNING

RESTRICTED
WILDLIFE AREA

FOR NEXT 5 MILES PHOTOGRAPHY
AND OBSERVATION OF WILDLIFE
PERMITTED FROM ROAD ONLY

NO HIKING OFF RO

Marking Territory

During the warm summer months, bears **shed** their winter fur coats. They also scratch and rub their bodies on structures to leave their scent and to mark their territories. They commonly use trees as rubbing posts. If there are no trees available, bears sometimes rub their backs on signposts.

Ready, Set, Go!

Grizzly bears have powerful shoulders. Their muscles allow them to burst with speed for short periods of time. Bears have been known to **run** up to thirty-five miles per hour!

Buckets of Berries

In late summer, the tundra and mountain slopes gradually turn to shades of crimson, yellow, and gold. Berries ripen across Alaska. Grizzly and brown bears have special lips that are well adapted for gathering berries off the bushes. Their large, supple lips extend away from their teeth so they can easily grasp and scoop the berries into their mouths.

Coastal brown bears love to feast on salmonberries, elderberries, highbush cranberries, and blueberries.

In Interior Alaska and the Arctic, grizzly bears also eat a variety of ripe, **sugary berries**. Some of their favorites include blueberries, soapberries, crowberries, and cranberries. When people pick berries, they have to be careful not to surprise a bear that might be thrashing through the bushes nearby.

Feast and Sleep

After a big meal of salmon and berries, it's time to rest. Bears like to dig out **day beds** or belly pits. Some bears choose shaded areas in the soft, mossy forest. They roll on their backs and stretch their legs toward the sky. Other times, they drop their full bellies into a shallow pit and lie facedown to digest their food.

A mother bear can become a perfect pillow for a sleepy cub.

Wild and Free

Alaska offers a special wilderness home for more than 30,000 grizzly and brown bears. Many other animals such as black bears, wolves, caribou, moose, and Dall sheep depend on Alaska's wild, open spaces to live healthy lives. Visitors come from all over the world to see the beauty of Alaska's wilderness and its great diversity of animals. If we **protect** places like Denali National Park and Katmai National Park, these magnificent bears will continue to **thrive**, wild and free, for many years to come.

Range of Grizzly & Brown Bears

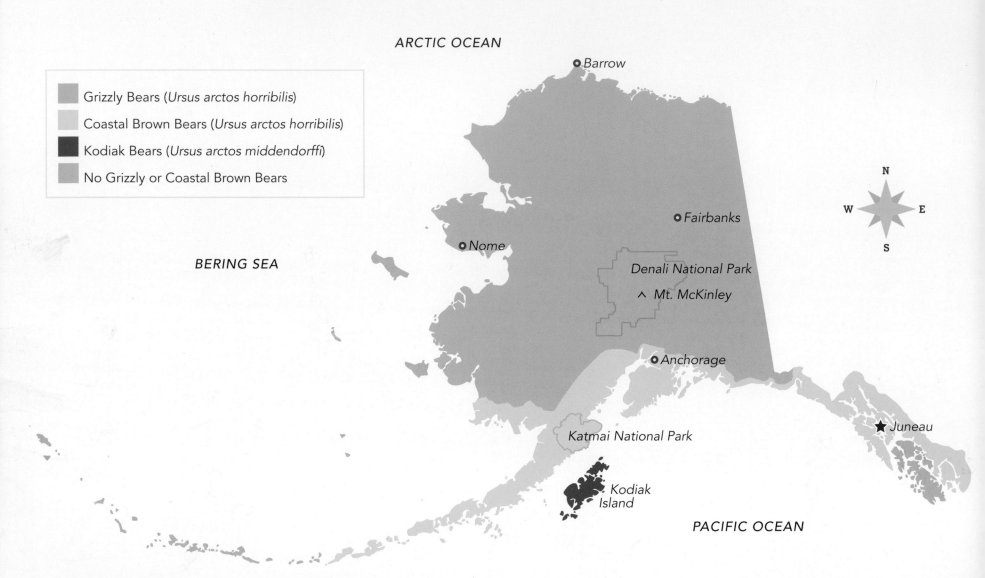

ARCTIC OCEAN

Legend:
- Grizzly Bears (*Ursus arctos horribilis*)
- Coastal Brown Bears (*Ursus arctos horribilis*)
- Kodiak Bears (*Ursus arctos middendorffi*)
- No Grizzly or Coastal Brown Bears

Barrow

Fairbanks

Nome

Denali National Park

∧ Mt. McKinley

Anchorage

BERING SEA

N
W   E
S

Katmai National Park

Kodiak Island

Juneau

PACIFIC OCEAN

Alaska

Grizzly and brown bears are the same species. This map illustrates the difference in their habitats, though their territory does overlap as bears roam freely across Alaska.

Alaska is also home to black bears and polar bears. It is the only state where all three species of bears in North America are found.

For Tom Campion. Thank you for your passion to protect Alaska's wilderness for the bears and other creatures tha[t] share this great land. —Debbie

Many thanks to Harry Reynolds, John Schoen, Richard Shidel[e] Roy Wood, Ed Weiss, Joe Meehan, Pat Owen, and Larry Aumi[ller]

Manufactured in China by Midas Printing International Ltd. (Hong Kong), in January 2014

Published by Little Bigfoot, an imprint of Sasquatch Books
18 17 16 15 14   9 8 7 6 5 4 3 2 1

Editor: Christy Cox
Project editor: Em Gale
Photographs: Patrick J. Endres
Cover design: Anna Goldstein
Interior Design/Map: Kitri Wood

Library of Congress Cataloging-in-Publication Data is available.

ISBN: 13- 978-1-57061-932-8 (paperback)
ISBN: 13- 978-1-57061-948-9 (hardcover)

Sasquatch Books
1904 Third Avenue, Suite 710
Seattle, WA 98101
(206) 467-4300
www.sasquatchbooks.com
custserv@sasquatchbooks.com

Get More Out of This Book

GROUP DISCUSSION

Lead a discussion about the text in the book:

 Ask readers to name the different types of bears found in Alaska. How many species of bears are there in North America? What are two characteristics of the grizzly that would enable someone to identify them?

 Did readers learn anything new about bears? Do they know any bear facts that weren't discussed in the book? How would they describe the grizzly bears—magnificent, fascinating, or terrifying? How does the author feel about grizzly bears? How can readers tell how the author feels?

Lead a discussion about the photographs in the book:

 Ask readers what they think the photographer was feeling as he observed the bears. Do they think that would be an interesting job, or would it be too scary?

 Do the bears in the photographs look friendly or mean? Is it better for a nonfiction book to have photographs instead of drawings? Show readers a familiar book with a fictional bear in it. Does seeing a cartoon picture of a bear make them less "real" or less scary?

Lead a discussion about Alaska:

 Have any readers been to Alaska, or lived there? Did they see any bears in the wild? Did they see any other Alaskan animals? Have they seen any of the Alaskan animals from the book in their local zoo?

 What do the photographs tell them about the climate and geography of Alaska? How is the state different from the one where they live?

INDEPENDENT ACTIVITIES

Have readers choose one of the following topics, do research, and write a report. And then present orally:

 Some of the animal food sources for the grizzly bear are voles, lemmings, Arctic ground squirrel, and caribou. Choose one of these animals to learn about.

 Protecting national parks is an important way to ensure that grizzly bears will continue to thrive in the wild. Choose one of the two National Parks in the book, Denali or Katmai, and learn more about it.

Have readers choose one of the following to write about:

 Why is it important, for animals and people, to protect wilderness areas like those in Alaska?

 Choose a photograph from the book and write an original story from their imagination about what is happening in the scene.

TEACHER'S GUIDE

The above discussion questions and activities are from our teacher's guide, which is aligned to the Common Core State Standards for English Language Arts for Grades 1 to 2. For the complete guide and a list of the exact standards it aligns with, visit our website: SasquatchBooks.com

A Garland of Games & Other Diversions

A GARLAND OF GAMES
& Other Diversions

An Alphabet Book

by Barbara Cooney

INITIAL LETTERS BY SUZANNE R. MORSE

COLONIAL WILLIAMSBURG

Williamsburg, Virginia

Distributed by

HOLT, RINEHART AND WINSTON, INC.

New York

For Jeanie and Margie

HOLT, RINEHART AND WINSTON SBN: 03-081016-7 (TRADE); SBN: 03-081017-5 (HLE)

COLONIAL WILLIAMSBURG SBN: 910412-01-4 (TRADE); SBN: 910412-02-2 (HLE)

Distributed simultaneously in Canada by Holt, Rinehart and Winston of Canada, Limited

Printed in the United States of America

A wicked Archer with cruel Arrow
Shot and killed a little sparrow.

B

Billie Boy, you are such trouble!
Come sit with me and Blow a Bubble.

Girls are good. They never tire
Of playing Cat's Cradle by the fire.

C

D

Girls love Dolls, and girls love Dances.
They flutter fans and give shy glances.

Emily in the parlor Embroiders neatly
While Hannah plays and Ann sings sweetly.

E

A-Fishing in the river, Billie caught an eel
That was much too long and lively to fit into his creel.

G

The Girls have Geese, whose quills make pens.
And for eggs they keep fat hens.

H

Boys go Hunting for turtles and 'possums,
While girls are Hunting for berries and blossoms.

In winter they skate on the pond if there's Ice.
Never skate if there isn't is good advice.

I

J

Jonquils and Jump-ropes come in the spring.
Pop goes the weasel, and mockingbirds sing.

People fly Kites and play King I am,
And Kitty saw Billie Kissing his Pam.

K

L

There are Lilacs and Leap-frog and—please, don't push—
Here we go 'round the Mulberry bush.

Marbles in a ring and Marbles in a hole,
Mumblety-peg, Mud-pies, and a Maypole.

M

N

There are dozens and dozens of games to play.

Here we come gathering Nuts in May.

Oranges and lemons, say the bells of St. Clemens.
Choose whom you wish, boys, girls, men and women.

P

Fair time arrives with chases for Pigs,
Prizes for fiddlers, broadswords and jigs.

Quoits on the green and Quarter-mile races,
Ladies in muslins and men in fine laces.

R

The gentlemen Ride and the children Run
To see the Rope dancer and join the fun.

Seesaws and Swings, battledores, Shuttlecocks,
All in the garden with pompous peacocks.

T

Boys peg their Tops; girls play at Tag,
While the governor plays at being a wag.

Up, Up goes the swing, feet in the leaves.
How high shall I push you? As high as you please.

U

V

Across the field and over by the pond
I found a Valentine from one of whom I'm fond.

He's made me a Whistle, a Willow Whistle too.

I don't know how to thank him, but I think a kiss will do.

I stepped into a boat on that very same pond,
And took a wee eXcursion with the one of whom I'm fond.

It was only a little boat, hardly a Yacht,
But the captain was my darling and he loved me a lot.

Zed, unfortunately, is Zed, which is the same as Z,
So it's up the wooden hill and into bed for me.